IMAGES
of America

LEOMINSTER FIREFIGHTING

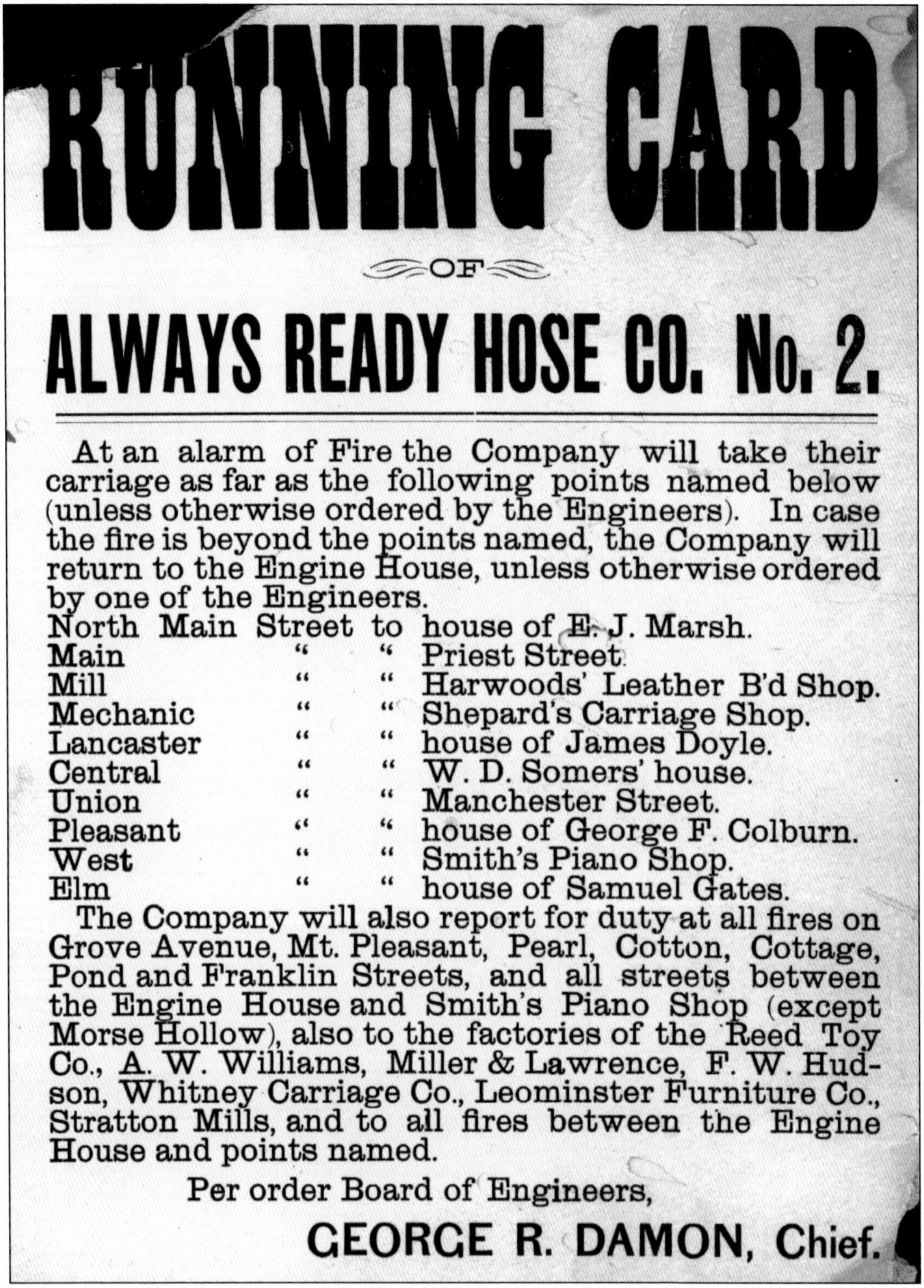

RUNNING CARD

OF

ALWAYS READY HOSE CO. No. 2.

At an alarm of Fire the Company will take their carriage as far as the following points named below (unless otherwise ordered by the Engineers). In case the fire is beyond the points named, the Company will return to the Engine House, unless otherwise ordered by one of the Engineers.

North Main Street to house of E. J. Marsh.
Main " " Priest Street.
Mill " " Harwoods' Leather B'd Shop.
Mechanic " " Shepard's Carriage Shop.
Lancaster " " house of James Doyle.
Central " " W. D. Somers' house.
Union " " Manchester Street.
Pleasant " " house of George F. Colburn.
West " " Smith's Piano Shop.
Elm " " house of Samuel Gates.

The Company will also report for duty at all fires on Grove Avenue, Mt. Pleasant, Pearl, Cotton, Cottage, Pond and Franklin Streets, and all streets between the Engine House and Smith's Piano Shop (except Morse Hollow), also to the factories of the Reed Toy Co., A. W. Williams, Miller & Lawrence, F. W. Hudson, Whitney Carriage Co., Leominster Furniture Co., Stratton Mills, and to all fires between the Engine House and points named.

Per order Board of Engineers,

GEORGE R. DAMON, Chief.

This 1880 running card for Hose Company 2 was discovered under the leg of the pool table at the Church Street fire station in 1990 during spring cleaning. Each of the hose companies was assigned a certain district in the town to respond to in the event of a fire. (Author's collection.)

On the cover: Members of Hose Company 2 pose outside the Church Street fire station at the beginning of the 20th century. (Courtesy of Leominster Firefighters Relief Association.)

IMAGES *of America*

LEOMINSTER FIREFIGHTING

Roger H. LaPointe

ARCADIA PUBLISHING

ISBN 978-0-7385-7209-3

Published by Arcadia Publishing
Charleston, South Carolina

Printed in the United States of America

Library of Congress Control Number: 2009927730

For all general information contact Arcadia Publishing at:
Telephone 843-853-2070
Fax 843-853-0044
E-mail sales@arcadiapublishing.com
For customer service and orders:
Toll-Free 1-888-313-2665

Visit us on the Internet at www.arcadiapublishing.com

This book is dedicated to all the former Leominster firefighters
for their selfless dedication to protect the community,
and to their families who waited for their safe return.

Contents

ACKNOWLEDGMENTS

Since I began my research in 1986, I have had the honor of meeting many former firefighters and family members who took the time to share with me their personal memories. I wish to express my deepest admiration and appreciation to the following who have shared with me their memories of a family member, including Larry Mitchell, Russell Johnson, Lora (Marquis) Lanza, Mae (Legault) Mitchell, Dennis Rosa, Raymond Morse, Eleanor (Ordway) King, and especially George and Mildred (Cutter) Hirst for the use of her father's personal diary.

I must acknowledge several retired firefighters who shared the good old days with me: call firefighter Anthony Amico, Deputy Chief William Ashton, Lt. Peter Cascio, Cliff Eldridge, Chief Frederick W. Johnson, call firefighter Rollin Lane Jr., Lt. Joe Love, Jeff Olson, Marcel Remy, Deputy Chief Robert Rheault, Chief Alfred LeBlanc, Lt. Robert Sideleau, Lt. James Surovich, Deputy Chief William "Tex" Thibodeau, Lt. Robert Thomas, and Deputy Chief Robert Halloran. A special thank-you goes to retired fire alarm operator Paul F. Kennedy for sharing a part of his collection.

I am deeply grateful to the staff at the Leominster Historical Society and the Leominster Historical Commission, especially Rocco Palmieri and Linda Pinder for the incredible amount of help with the collection of glass negatives of Edmund G. Davis and Percy Johnson and to those at the Leominster Public Library and the staff at the Fitchburg Historical Society for opening their doors to me.

I must also thank the following departed firefighters for the many cups of coffee and their sharing of stories: Vincent Tremblay, Larry Amico, Deputy Chief Ross Amico, Bill Penning and Emidio Martini, and especially Uncle George Boisvert for allowing me to come and visit him so many times in fire alarm after school and my mentor and dear friend firefighter Roger Bigelow.

Finally and most importantly, I extend my deepest gratitude to my dad for taking me to all those fires as a young child during his call firefighter days and to my mother for letting him. And to my wife Debbie and two sons, Bryan and Scott, I must say thank you for all your support and encouragement. I could not have done it without you all!

INTRODUCTION

It was in 1820 when the townspeople of Leominster took up a subscription "in the interests of protecting the rights of the settlers in case of fire." In that year, two hand engines were purchased and designated simply Engine Company 1 and Engine Company 2. These first companies set 15 rules, which included that "each member must have two fire buckets with the first letter and surname on it and it must be kept in a handy place at home." At the sounding of church bells, the men would grab their engines and race to the scene. Bucket brigades would be formed to carry water to these engines, and the machines would be "pumped" to put a stream of water onto the fire.

In July 1846, the town purchased of the W. C. Hunneman Company of Boston its first water engine, which was named Torrent Engine Company 1. Another engine, designated the Union 2, was purchased for the North Village in 1848. These hand engines required that each company have 60 men to operate them efficiently. Four shifts of 12 men, 6 men on each side of the machine, four rows deep, pumping furiously in 15 to 20 seconds and in a split second, the next 6 men would take over. They would have to wait until 1866, when rubber coats were first purchased for the use of the firefighters.

It would not be until May 1868 that the town created a board of engineers to formally organize a fire department. The firefighters were paid $5 per year for their services. Leominster purchased a steam fire engine in 1870, which helped greatly in aiding the firefighters in getting water onto the fire quickly. With the addition of fire hydrants, used for the first time in November 1873, the "old hand tubs" were disbanded, and four hose companies created in their place: the Monoosnoc, Always Ready, George J. King, and Torrent. As time passed, there came the Washington, Combination, and Franklin.

As the town continued to grow, a ladder company also became necessary, and in 1867, the men of the department, most being tradesmen, built their own hook and ladder wagon, christened the *Junior*. As the years went by and new ladder wagons were purchased, they would change their name to the Babcock, Young Americans, Wachusett, Independent, Hardscrabble, Excelsior, and Clipper.

The first alarm on the new Stevens Electric Fire Alarm was received on September 12, 1891. Prior to the installation of this system, firefighters relied on the sounding of an alarm on the town bell. "If in a northerly direction from the Town Hall, two strokes will be given, a pause and then repeated. If in a southerly direction, three strokes; if east, four strokes and if west five strokes. To call the Fire Department of the North Village a second general alarm will be given."

By the 20th century, there was a need for a more permanent department, and in June 1904, they appointed their first permanent firefighter. In 1912, the first motorized apparatus arrived, motor hose 5, and thus the end of the horse-drawn era began. By 1920, Leominster had grown into a city and formed a permanent department with two platoons working an 84-hour workweek. Leominster firefighters were given their first instructions in rendering first aid on March 8, 1928, when Dr. Grant F. Hartzell of John Hopkins Hospital of Baltimore visited. But it was not until 1946 that the department paid the Ellis Fire Appliance Company $175 for one Scott Air-pak with mask. When it arrived, the members greeted this "new technology" that would allow them to enter smoke-filled atmospheres safely.

There have been more than 1,400 individuals who have served as members of the Leominster Fire Department since its beginning in 1820, and in nearly every memorable moment in history, they have left their mark. During the influenza epidemic of 1918, which took the lives of more than a half million people in this country, a young firefighter by the name of Paul Corey of Hose Company 3 died from that tragic illness.

These firefighters were war veterans who served their country nobly. They were part of nearly every memorable battle in time, seeing battle at Fredericksburg, Normandy, the Battle of the Bulge, Okinawa, Korea, and Vietnam. They were heroes, receiving the Bronze Star, the Silver Star, the Purple Heart, and numerous battle stars and presidential citations. And there was a young man, firefighter Clifton LeDuc of Hose Company 4, who answered the call to duty in World War I and died as a result of injuries he received while in Europe.

They rode on horseback with the Vermont Mounted Volunteers; they were Seabees; they were members of the Parachute Infantry; there are those who served aboard the USS *Wabash*, the USS *Yorktown*, and USS *Lexington*; and there were tank commanders, air force pilots, and the "chosen few." These firefighters have served in every war: the Civil War, Spanish-American War, World Wars I and II, the Korean War, Vietnam, and Iraq. They were members of the U.S. Army, U.S. Navy, U.S. Air Force, U.S. Marines, U.S. Coast Guard, and state and national guards.

These firefighters also shared a commitment to serve Leominster, joining fraternal organizations such as the Eagles, the Elks, the Knights of Columbus, and the St. Jean de Baptiste. They were Masons, Odd Fellows, and Rotarians. And in 1954, they began a partnership with the Muscular Dystrophy Association to bring aid and relief to children fighting that disease.

The Leominster firefighters are proud of the history and traditions that have been given to them. I have learned of their deeds and heroism and in doing so have gained a great deal of respect and admiration for these firefighters and their families. In *Leominster Firefighting*, I hope to share with you these acts, and in that way, their legacy will live on.

One

The Early Years

In July 1846, Leominster purchased its first water engine from the Hunneman Company of Boston. Christened the *Torrent*, "it was a plain tub machine, without bell or buckets and destitute of ornament." A company of 60 men was needed to operate it efficiently; four shifts of 12 men pumping in 15-second intervals to create a stream that could reach upwards of 178 feet. (Courtesy of Robert Rheault.)

In January 1873, the town purchased an engine for the Union Company in the North Village. It was a squirrel tail (named for the way the hose lay on top) built by the Hunneman Company at a cost of $1,750. The 1848 Union 2, which is now owned by the Leominster Firefighter Relief Association (LFRA), replaced the 1846 *Torrent* in town because it was in poor condition. (Courtesy of Paul F. Kennedy.)

The men of the department, many being craftsmen by trade, realized a need for a ladder company, and in 1867, they assembled their first ladder wagon and named it the Junior Hook and Ladder Company 1. The carriage was purchased from the C. W. Durant Company and was fitted with 96 feet of assorted ladders, four buckets, two axes, and hooks. (Courtesy of LFRA collection.)

In 1870, the department purchased a second-class steam fire engine from the Amoskeag Manufacturing Company of Manchester, New Hampshire, and it was given the name of the *Aurora*. It cost $5,571 and weighed 6,270 pounds. The steamer remained in service until 1927 when it was turned over to the highway department. (Photograph by E. G. Davis; courtesy of the Leominster Historical Society.)

On August 1, 1870, the members of the Torrent Engine Company and the hook and ladder company took possession of their new engine house on Church Street, opposite the present-day station. It was built of brick, measured 60 feet by 40 feet, and was two stories high, with room for two engines and a hook and ladder and reception rooms for each company. The total cost of the new station was $8,208.43 (Courtesy of LFRA collection.)

The members of Monoosnoc Hose Company 1 take a moment to proudly show off their hose wagon in Monument Square. It was manufactured by the Amoskeag Manufacturing Company of Manchester, New Hampshire, at a cost of $620 and arrived in June 1871. In September 1871, Charles A. Wheelock, the assistant foreman, was killed when he fell from a train. (Photograph by E. G. Davis; courtesy of the Leominster Historical Society.)

During the summer of 1873, the brave lads of the North Village organized the Young Americans Hook and Ladder Company. It consisted of only young boys, whose average age was 15 years old. On November 1, 1873, they challenged the men of the Junior Hook and Ladder Company from the center to a muster trial and won. (Photograph by E. G. Davis; courtesy of the Leominster Historical Society.)

The members of the department have turned out for this photograph in the mid-1870s, dressed in uniform for the annual parade. The Aurora and Monoosnoc Hose Company 1 would take part in trials against the fire companies from the North Village each year for a prized cup and bragging rights. Firefighters were paid $15 per year for their services. (Courtesy of LFRA collection.)

A photograph was taken in the spring of 1880 of the Washington Hose Company 1. It was reported in the *Leominster Enterprise* newspaper that "a photo of the hose carriage with horses attached occupies a large oval in the center, with individual photographs of the company in small ovals around it." The company's motto was "Deeds, not Words." The carriage was built by Amoskeag Manufacturing Company and carried 1,000 feet of hose. (Author's collection.)

In October 1879, members of the Hardscrabble Hook and Ladder Company 1, in the center, set an unprecedented time of 1 minute and 17.5 seconds during a muster trial and were declared the "Champions of all New England if not the U.S." They then formed a new company under the name of the Excelsior Hook and Ladder Company and sent out a challenge to any company in the state or the world to a competition for a purse of $100. The challenge went unanswered. Their time had never before and never would be matched and was quite an achievement. This was such an achievement that they were seldom invited to a muster in other towns. The truck was built by the Babcock Extinguisher Company of New York. The foreman was Hebert E. Woods, the assistant foreman was Charles H. Bennett, and the clerk was Elmer H. Bates. The remaining members were Frank Joy, Charles Nutter, Lewis Bates, William Cole, George Edgerly, Charles Bennett, O. C. Gibson, E. R. Tisdale, G. F. Sanderson, Elmer Philips, Henry Orcutt, Fred Morse, C. B. Smith, Fred Harrington, Wallace Jewett, and C. H. Joslin. (Courtesy of LFRA collection.)

On March 22, 1865, Kendall Hall was dedicated for the North Village. It was built as a town hall and a schoolhouse and was also used as a library and police lockup. In September 1889, the fire department took over the lower floor and closed the Union Station on Main Street. The department continues to operate from this location at Hamilton and Main Streets. (Courtesy of the Leominster Historical Society.)

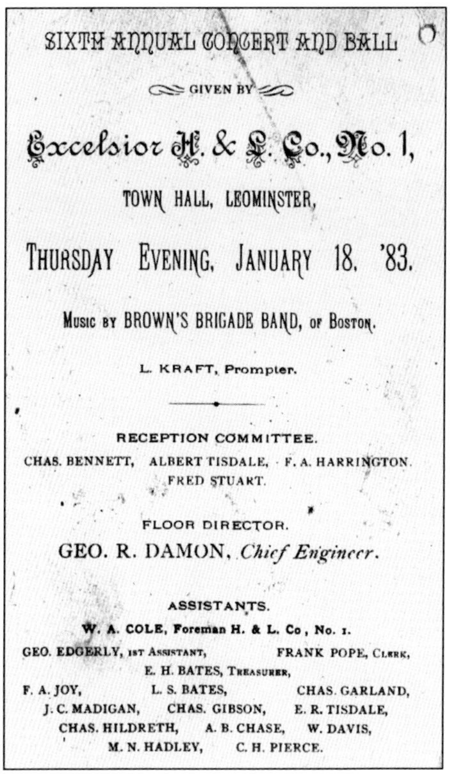

SIXTH ANNUAL CONCERT AND BALL

GIVEN BY

Excelsior H. & L. Co., No. 1,

TOWN HALL, LEOMINSTER,

THURSDAY EVENING, JANUARY 18, '83.

MUSIC BY BROWN'S BRIGADE BAND, OF BOSTON.

L. KRAFT, Prompter.

RECEPTION COMMITTEE.

CHAS. BENNETT, ALBERT TISDALE, F. A. HARRINGTON, FRED STUART.

FLOOR DIRECTOR.

GEO. R. DAMON, *Chief Engineer*.

ASSISTANTS.

W. A. COLE, Foreman H. & L. Co, No. 1.

GEO. EDGERLY, 1ST ASSISTANT, FRANK POPE, CLERK,

E. H. BATES, TREASURER,

F. A. JOY, L. S. BATES, CHAS. GARLAND,

J. C. MADIGAN, CHAS. GIBSON, E. R. TISDALE,

CHAS. HILDRETH, A. B. CHASE, W. DAVIS,

M. N. HADLEY, C. H. PIERCE.

A concert and ball on January 18, 1883, was given by the Excelsior Hook and Ladder Company. Each fire company would hold its own concert, and the money raised was used to adorn carriages or to purchase much-needed equipment and uniforms for the members. Any remaining money was left in the treasury and divided by its members at the end of the year. (Courtesy of LFRA collection.)

In 1895, it was voted to do away with Franklin Hose 3 and the Wachusett Hook and Ladder 2 and combine the two to form one company. The town contracted with H. F. Keyes of Clinton for a combination hose and ladder wagon. The Franklin Hose 3 and Combination Hose 2 wagons were sold in 1914 to Providence, Rhode Island, for the sum of $2,000. (Courtesy of Paul F. Kennedy.)

The hose reel belonging to Franklin Hose 3 was discovered in the basement of Kendall Hall and restored by the members of the department. The firefighters of the late 1800s would pull the cart by hand and, using the Union engine, lay a line to put out the fire. It now sports a large firefighter's boot and can be seen at any Muscular Dystrophy Association (MDA) event. (Photograph by Robert Rheault.)

A Hayes aerial ladder truck with tiller was purchased in 1892 and named the *Clipper*. It was built by the LaFrance Fire Engine Company and carried 105 feet of ladders in addition to its 65-foot aerial, which was raised by cranks. The truck proved to be too heavy to be pulled and was traded to East Providence, Rhode Island, in 1901. (Photograph by E. G. Davis; courtesy of the Leominster Historical Society.)

Members of the ladder company practice before a muster in this 1904 photograph. The event was one in which the 12 members would set their carriage, run from a position 40 rods away, pull their carriage the 40 rods, splice ladders together, and put a man on the roof. In the lower portion are Capt. Ernest C. Trimnell and firefighter Nathaniel Lowe. (Courtesy of Dorothy Shepard.)

The central fire station located at 19 Church Street was opened to the inspection of the public with a grand opening on March 15, 1898. A large crowd gathered that afternoon, and as reported in the *Leominster Enterprise*, "the sliding poles, which connect the sleeping rooms to those below attracted much attention and were tried by everyone but the ladies." The inside of the lower floors were painted a rose color, and the upper rooms were each decorated by the respective hose companies, each of them having their own flair. That evening, Selectman Augustus L. Whitney made a short speech and presented the keys to Chief Charles A. Garland. It cost $21,508.02. (Photograph by E. G. Davis; courtesy of the Leominster Historical Society.)

This photograph of the interior of the Church Street fire station at the beginning of the 20th century shows the harnesses at the ready as they hang from the ceiling. In the rear, the horse stalls can be seen. At the sound of an alarm, the doors would open, the horses would take their place in front of their wagons, and the harnesses would be lowered. (Courtesy of LFRA collection.)

The firefighters of the hook and ladder company stand ready in uniform for the annual parade in 1905 at the rear of the town hall with the 1901 Seagraves city service truck. It carried 286 feet of ladders and weighed 4,600 pounds. Lt. Walter F. O' Brien stands at far left, and Capt. Ernest C. Trimnell stands third from left. (Courtesy of James McCoy.)

The steamer is seen here on Church Street alongside the Baptist church in this photograph taken by noted photographer E. G. Davis. The steamer gave more than 57 years of service to the fire department and was turned over to the highway department in 1927. It was reportedly scrapped in the 1940s for the war effort. (Courtesy of the Leominster Historical Society.)

The Combination Hose Company 2 horse-drawn wagon stands outside the Lancaster Street fire station with firefighter John Mellin. Located at 145 Lancaster Street, it was designated as Station 3 and responded to all calls on the south side of Leominster. It was built at a cost of $13,000 and opened on September 18, 1909. It was abandoned in 1966. (Photograph by Percy Johnson; courtesy of the Leominster Historical Commission.)

The board of engineers was chosen by the selectmen of the town and was responsible in forming each of the companies needed to protect its citizens. In this photograph from 1913 is the city's first permanent chief, Frederick A. Russell, seated in the center. To his left is Assistant Chief Engineer Ernest H. Phelps, and to his right is Assistant Chief Engineer Fredson N. Gray. (Courtesy of Barbara Bigelow.)

The members of Hose Company 2 pose for this photograph from the mid-1920s, outside the Lancaster Street station with the 1917 White pump and the combination hose wagon. Pictured are, from left to right, Louis G. Miller and Carl Tyler (drivers), Capt. Phillip Cloutier, Thomas Regan, Fred L. Gleason, Louis Valiton, Archie Marquis, Joseph Vacha, Arthur Robichaud, Lawrence Lundigan, Lt. Adolphus Miller, Harry Manchester, and unidentified. (Courtesy of LFRA collection.)

Two

FROM HORSE DRAWN TO HORSEPOWER

In March 1912, Leominster received its first motorized piece of apparatus, a Boyd costing $5,500. Firefighter William McCauley was appointed as the driver. Seated beside him is Chief Fred Russell, with Capt. Richard H. Cutter and firefighter Harry Manchester on the rear of the truck. This vehicle was destroyed one year later when it was struck by a train at the Mechanic Street crossing. (Courtesy of Mildred Hirst.)

The town purchased the E.M.F. Flanders chief's car for the price of $790 from M. Faulk. It arrived in October 1912 and was equipped with a 35-gallon chemical tank and 200 feet of three-quarter-inch hose. Chief Frederick A. Russell was the first driver. It was brought to Taunton in 1927. (Courtesy of Robert Rheault.)

In 1914, the new Boyd 4, a model C, arrived to replace the one destroyed by the train. The permanent members of the department are seen here. They are, from left to right, Capt. Richard H. Cutter, Walter Cushing, Lester Harrington, and Lt. George LaBuff. The driver is Carl Stannard. On the truck are, from left to right, Nathaniel Lowe, Clarence King, Myron Lamb, Olia Kirby, Ward H. Kennedy, and Harry Manchester. (Courtesy of LFRA collection.)

The North Leominster firefighters received their first motorized apparatus, also a Boyd, in 1915. They are seen here posing outside the station around 1923. In the photograph are Albert Souther (left), William Beard (fourth from left), and Capt. Alfred Stone (far right). Standing on the rear of the truck is Timothy Crowley. Seated on top are Raymond B. Lancey and unidentified. The driver is Frank E. Wilson. (Courtesy of Larry Mitchell.)

The 1917 White delivered on January 27 was a six-cylinder pump car equipped with a Rumsey Rotary 750-gallon-per-minute pump and was Leominster's first pumping engine. Designated engine 1, it carried a 35-gallon chemical tank, 200 feet of three-quarter-inch hose, 1,000 feet of three-inch hose, and other equipment. It was built by O. F. Kress and Sons and cost $6,500. (Courtesy of Mildred Hirst.)

Leominster bought its first motorized ladder truck in 1918. It was produced by the White Motor Company, cost $7,844, and was purchased from O. F. Kress Company of Lawrence. It carried 394 feet of ladders and weighed 13,000 pounds. In the 1950s, it was decommissioned, and the chassis was put into Spec Pond to be used as a base for a wharf. (Courtesy of LFRA collection.)

In May 1922, the city purchased a White triple pumper. Designated engine 1, it had a four-cylinder engine and cost $9,655. This photograph, taken on June 10, 1923, shows the members of Hose Company 1. From left to right are Walter Lynch, George Small, Maurice Hardy, Walter Cushing, Francis Lamb, Charles Hubbard, Lt. Fred Lynch, and Capt. G. Artelle Wass. The drivers are Osia Legault and Honorat Comeau. (Courtesy of LFRA collection.)

The members of Hose Company 2 pose outside the Lancaster Street station in the mid-1920s with the 1917 White pump, which was renamed engine 2. From left to right are Arthur Robichaud, Joseph Vacha, Paul Tourigny, Lawrence Lundigan, Archie Marquis, Fred Gleason, Louis Valiton, Thomas Regan, and Capt. Phillip Cloutier. Seated are, from left to right, Carl Tyler and Louis Miller. (Courtesy of Lora Lanza.)

November 1927 saw the addition of the Ahrens Fox. The 750-gallon-per-minute pump cost $12,000. In the front seat are, from left to right, Alfred J. Morse and Honorat Comeau. Standing are, from left to right, Charles W. Hirst, Albert N. Anderson, Maurice F. Hardy, Francis Lamb, Osias Legault, Walter Cushing, and Capt. Walter E. Lynch. (Courtesy of Vincent Anderson.)

Firefighter Nathaniel Lowe was one of the drivers assigned to the Buffalo when it arrived on September 7, 1933. At the time, it was the most modern piece of fire apparatus to date. A special 600-gallon triple combination pump with booster, it was loaded with 1,400 feet of two-and-a-half-inch hose. The cost was $8,125. (Courtesy of Paul F. Kennedy.)

On November 18, 1934, the department received its second Buffalo and put it into service at North Leominster. The city paid $9,124.37 to the Buffalo Fire Appliance Corporation for one Buffalo type 7RR, 750-gallon, triple combination pump, booster, and hose car. It had a Waukesha engine and a Hale rotary pump. Firefighter Aime Rheault is pictured in the driver's seat. (Courtesy of Robert Rheault.)

The Seagraves, an 85-foot, four-section aerial ladder truck, arrived on February 5, 1946. Costing the city $18,438.70, it was powered by a 240-horsepower V-12 engine. It saw its first action at a fire on the third floor of Toolin's three-story block at 237 Water Street on March 17. Firefighter Osias "Pete" Legault, seen here, was the driver. (Courtesy of Mae Legault Mitchell.)

On May 21, 1951, a GMC chassis was purchased from Todd and Fiske for $4,227. After being fitted as a city service ladder truck, its final cost was $9,332. The work was done by William C. Moore of Boylston. Pictured are, from left to right, Leo Enright, Lt. Rosario Amico, Alvin Hembrow, William Wheeler, Pete Angelini, Joe Love, and Roland Peloquin. (Courtesy of LFRA collection.)

The duties of the firefighters would expand in May 1952 with the arrival of the department's first ambulance. The Cadillac was purchased from Meteor Sales of New England for $6,260. The department had always been relied upon to provide emergency medicine and called to Leominster Hospital with the "lungmotor" to resuscitate those patients who had succumbed to illness and death. (Courtesy of Paul F. Kennedy.)

Engine 4, the 1952 FWD, is shown operating in the front of the Eagle Block on Mechanic Street at a general-alarm fire in 1962. Purchased from E. F. Edson Company, the 750-gallon-per-minute pump had four-wheel drive and cost $12,596. It would eventually be sold to the Town of Princeton. (Courtesy of William Ashton.)

This Ford, delivered on April 4, 1955, was designated engine 6 and had a 600-gallon water tank. The class A, 500-gallon-per-minute pump carried an electric booster line reel, over 1,500 feet of two-and-a-half-inch hose, and a 32-foot, three-section metal ladder. It was the first time that metal ladders were placed on trucks. It was purchased from Boylston Fire Equipment and cost $4,369. (Courtesy of LFRA collection.)

On November 29, 1956, the new FWD engine 2 arrived from Clintonsville, Wisconsin. A 1,000-gallon-per-minute pump, it was four-wheel drive and cost $17,939. It also contained a 500-gallon water tank with preconnected hose lines. It was later designated engine 5 and served in North Leominster until its recent retirement. (Courtesy of Paul F. Kennedy.)

The 1951 GMC ladder was sent to West Boylston in July 1957 and fitted with a 65-foot electric aerial at a cost of $7,250. This truck was purchased by the Atlantic Union College and presented to the Town of Lancaster in 1967. (Courtesy of William Ashton.)

Chief Frederick W. Johnson stands proudly next to the new chief's car in 1960. The Pontiac was purchased for $2,745 from Hapgood Motors at 310 North Main Street and replaced the aging 1954 Buick. (Courtesy of LFRA collection.)

The fire department received a new Cadillac ambulance for its use on May 19, 1961. It was purchased from Leominster Motor Sales at a cost of $12,095 and put into service at 4:30 p.m. In the photograph are firefighters Marcel "Pete" Remy (left) and Francis Lucier. (Courtesy of George Boisvert.)

A new FWD, designated engine 3, arrived in August 1967. It had a 1,250-gallon-per-minute pump and cost $32,000. While responding to what was found to be a false alarm, on October 7, 1984, it lost a front wheel while rounding the corner from Main Street to Hawes Street. Fortunately, the three firefighters received only minor injuries. The truck was taken out of service permanently. (Courtesy of LFRA collection.)

In October 1967, a 100-foot aerial ladder, built by Maxim Motors of Middleboro, was delivered at a cost of $48,000. It carried, in addition to its aerial, 229 feet of ground ladders, forcible entry tools, and a lighting plant. It was tractor drawn with a tiller and at its time was the longest aerial ladder in all Worcester County outside of Worcester. (Courtesy of LFRA collection.)

In the 1970s, studies concluded that drivers could not see the color red, so fire trucks became lime yellow in color. On October 26, 1973, Leominster added its latest piece of apparatus, called the *Snorkel*, with a 55-foot boom at a cost of $65,332. Thankfully, in the early 1980s, the yellow was retired, and as the trucks were refurbished, they were painted the traditional red. (Photograph by Robert Rheault.)

Three

Faces

This photograph of three unidentified fire engineers in the mid-1880s shows that the firefighters of Leominster took pride in how they looked. One thing that is known from the numerous company journals is that each company purchased their own uniforms to be worn at company musters, the annual department parade, and when working at fires. (Photograph by E. G. Davis; courtesy of the Leominster Historical Society.)

In May 1867, the town selectmen appointed seven men who would form the first board of engineers. Immediately after being appointed, they would meet and vote as to who would serve as chief engineer as well as the order of assistants, and Emory Tilton was chosen as the first chief engineer for Leominster. He would remain as chief until October 16, 1873. (Courtesy of the Leominster Historical Society.)

George R. Damon served in the Civil War with Company A, the 36th Massachusetts Infantry and after being discharged on disability reentered as a corporal with Company E, the 5th Massachusetts infantry, seeing battle at Fredericksburg. He entered the fire department in 1867, served with the Torrent Engine Company, and would eventually serve 10 years as chief engineer of the department. (Courtesy of Leominster Historical Society.)

Albert W. Allen joined Company E, 1st Regiment of Vermont Mounted Volunteers in 1861 and rose to the rank of sergeant. In May 1873, he was named treasurer of the Junior Hook and Ladder Company. In the early 1880s, he transferred to the Torrent Hose Company, serving as clerk and eventually foreman. During his last few years, he served as a member of the board of engineers. (Courtesy of Leominster Historical Society.)

The Hardscrabble Hook and Ladder Company is seen in this photograph from 1878. From left to right are (first row) Charles Joslin, Charles Nutter, Elmer Bates, foreman Herbert Woods, assistant foreman Charles Bennett, Frank Joy, and O. Charles Gibson; (second row) Fred Morse, L. Saul Bates, Henry Orcutt, Wallace Jewett, Charles B. Smith, and Bradford Marden; (third row) Elmer Phillips, Charles H. Pierce, Fred Harrington, George Edgerly, and William Cole. (Courtesy of LFRA collection.)

Foreman James T. Killelea was one of many in the Killelea family to serve with the Leominster Fire Department. He began his career with the Always Ready Hose Company in the early 1880s. In 1885, he transferred to the Clipper Hook and Ladder Company and was assigned the extinguisher man. He left the department in 1899, after serving as foreman for nine years. (Courtesy of LFRA collection.)

Each year in May, the department formed its companies. In this 1888 photograph are the members of the Washington Hose Company 1. In the center is foreman Walter H. Rugg surrounded by John Madigan, treasurer; Ernest Perkins, assistant foreman; John Wilcox, clerk; Frank Gleason; Harry Donovan; William Wilcox; Edwin Hayward; Wilbur Sumner; and Harry Sawyer, steward. (Courtesy of the Leominster Historical Society.)

Frank J. Woodbury served as the clerk of the Hardscrabble Hook and Ladder Company in 1874 and moved to the Monoosnoc Hose Company 1 in 1875, which later became the Washington, serving as the foreman in 1882. In 1898, he was chosen as a member of the board of engineers where he remained until his death in 1907. He was a founding father of the LFRA in 1879. (Courtesy of LFRA collection.)

Charles A. Garland served more than 40 years with the department, beginning in 1882 with the ladder company. He would become a member of Torrent Hose Company in 1884 and rise through the ranks to captain in 1889. In 1892, he was chosen as a member of the board of engineers and chief in 1900. He also served as president of the Hose 4 Association for 28 years. (Courtesy of LFRA collection.)

William K. Morse was regarded as "one of the most efficient heads the fire service ever had." In 1895, he joined with the Combination Hose Company and became a member of the board of engineers in 1900. In 1905, he was elected as chief engineer. After leaving the fire service, he served with the 26th Division in France as the sergeant of Company D, 101st supply train. (Courtesy of Raymond Morse.)

Charles E. Murray was the driver of the Combination Hose Company 2, seen here in 1903, and later with Washington Hose Company 1, serving until 1911. On October 6, 1924, he entered into a manhole to rescue Michael Regan, a call firefighter who had become overcome by gas while working with the highway department, and both men were killed. Murray was recognized by the Carnegie Hero Fund. (Courtesy of LFRA collection.)

In 1904, a young man named Richard H. Cutter was appointed as the department's first permanent firefighter. He would eventually be made a permanent captain, the first and only in department history, and remained with the department until his retirement in 1946. His accomplishments included serving as the LFRA president for a period of 37 years, and the department's true historian. The duties of the officer included recording the fire calls and personnel on duty, and Captain Cutter was meticulous in his detailed reports of every change and event that occurred in the department's logbooks. He also kept a private journal, which is in the hands of the LFRA. (Courtesy of LFRA collection.)

Frederick A. Russell began his firefighting career with the Torrent Hose Company 4 in 1894. In 1909, he was appointed as a member of the board of engineers and chosen as the second engineer and clerk. In 1910, he was chosen as Leominster's first permanent fire chief and remained in that position until his retirement on June 4, 1922. (Courtesy of LFRA collection.)

In 1936, Harold S. Bailey became the first firefighter in the department to be appointed from a civil service exam when he was promoted to the rank of lieutenant. He entered the department in 1915 but left to serve with the U.S. Marines in 1917, returning in 1919. He retired in 1947 from injuries that he received from battling a fire on Spruce Street. (Courtesy of LFRA collection.)

Firefighter Raymond B. Lancey is the one and only firefighter in the history of the department to give his life in the line of duty. A member of Hose Company 3 in North Leominster, he was killed when a six-gallon fire extinguisher exploded on May 18, 1924, while firefighters were battling a brush fire near White's Pond that was threatening a number of cottages. According to the report filed by Capt. Richard H. Cutter, "he was leaning over the top of the extinguisher when the bottom blew out throwing him and the rest of the extinguisher about ten feet in the air. It was a brake bottle Babcock six gallon extinguisher and was charged with water, bi-carbonate of soda and sulfuric acid." The chemical reaction is capable of generating a pressure inside the bottle of 160 to 200 pounds per square inch, which in turn will force an effective stream of approximately 25 feet. He was only 22 years old. (Courtesy of Paul F. Kennedy.)

Ernest H. Phelps began his career with the Wachusett Hook and Ladder Company 2 in 1890 and served until it was disbanded in 1895, joining with Franklin Hose Company 3 in North Leominster. He served as a lieutenant in 1909 and became the assistant engineer in 1914. In 1923, he was appointed as chief and retired in 1932. (Courtesy of Barbara Bigelow.)

Appointed to Hose Company 4 as a call firefighter in 1912, Ernest P. Johnson's career spanned nearly 42 years. He was appointed a permanent firefighter in 1915 and promoted to the rank of lieutenant in 1922. He served as chief of the department from 1932 until his retirement in June 1954. He also served as treasurer of the LFRA from 1933 until 1952. (Courtesy of LFRA collection.)

Fred L. Gleason is seen in this photograph from the 1950s. He was first appointed to the department as a call firefighter in 1918, retiring in 1956. He was known as "Old Sarge" and carried the U.S. Marine Corps colors in parades for 62 years. As a youngster, he was a well-known boxer. (Courtesy of LFRA collection.)

Assistant Chief Engineer Everett Burnap is seen here in this 1954 photograph. He first joined the department in 1929 with Hose Company 3 in the village, rising to the rank of captain in 1934 and appointed to the board of engineers in 1948. He was one of the last of the "old time" engineers when he retired in 1964 after a 35-year career. (Courtesy of Paul F. Kennedy.)

At the end of 1940, the department consisted of 23 permanent firefighters, consisting of 1 chief and 11 men assigned to two platoons. They worked an 84-hour workweek: two day shifts of 10 hours each, followed by a full 24-hour shift, and then two 14-hour night shifts. They had the sixth day off. They were augmented by 41 call firefighters. Pictured here are the permanent firefighters of the city of Leominster in 1940. They are, from left to right, Fred Gleason, Maurice

Hardy, Carl Tyler, Louis Miller, Harry Mitchell, Nathaniel Lowe, Myron Lamb, Frank Wilson, William "Tom" Garland, Joseph Cormier, Capt. Richard H. Cutter, Chief Ernest Johnson, Lt. Harold Bailey, Adolphus Miller, Alfred Morse, Harold "Chet" Hildreth, Bernard Gray, Honorat Comeau, Albert Leighton, Clarence Bentley, Gordon Wilson, Elmer Clark, and Osias "Pete" Legault. (Courtesy of Ronald Pierce.)

On February 5, 1946, the Seagraves, an 85-foot, four-section aerial ladder truck, arrived. The call firefighters would answer the department whistles and report to the central fire station and await orders from the chief. Many of these men were with the electric light company, the gas company, and business owners who would leave their work place and assist the firefighters on duty. Pictured are, from left to right, engineer Royal Turner, Capt. Harry Battis, Al Girardin, Elmer Clark, George Schofield, Aime Rheault, Alfred Fournier, Alvin Hembrow, Ray Piper, James Skinner, Lester Rousseau, Emile Mailloux, Bernard Martin, and Felix Seliga. The driver is Osias Legault. When the 1967 Maxim ladder arrived, the Seagraves ladder remained in service until the mid-1980s when it was retired. (Courtesy of Mae Legault Mitchell.)

On January 1, 1952, the department changed from a two-platoon system working 84 hours a week to three platoons working 56 hours a week. A permanent firefighter's work schedule consisted of working three 10-hour day shifts followed by one day off and then continued with three 14-hour night shifts. They were then given two days off and would repeat the rotation. There were now 34 firefighters, 4 officers, and 38 call firefighters assigned to the department. Those firefighters appearing in this photograph are, from left to right, (first row) Eugene Davis, Leo LeBlanc, William Farnsworth, Lt. Joseph Cormier, Chief Ernest Johnson, Lt. James Skinner, Lt. Raymond Piper, Roger Robichaud, and Charles Lowe; (second row) Roger Caisse, Leopold Thibodeau, Rosario Amico, Donald Markham, Arthur Pike, Norman Valois, Paul Angelini, and Leo Enright; (third row) George Boisvert, Robert Sideleau, Bernard Martin, Felice Gabrieli, Fred Gleason, William Wheeler, and Luigi Barassi; (fourth row) Donald Gillis, Gordon Wilson, Robert Miller, Albert Girardin, and Aime Rheault. (Courtesy of Robert Rheault.)

Frederick W. Johnson was sworn in as chief of the department on May 25, 1954, by state representative Arthur O. Mahan (at right) as Mayor Ralph W. Crossman looks on. He entered the department in 1946 and was promoted to lieutenant in 1953, retiring in 1988 after 42 years. At the time of his appointment as chief, he was the youngest in the Commonwealth of Massachusetts. (Courtesy of LFRA collection.)

Lt. William Farnsworth (at left) and firefighter Alvin Hembrow are seen here after rescuing a dog from Rockwell's Pond in the late 1950s. Lieutenant Farnsworth suffered a heart attack while on vacation with his family and died at the age of 41 in October 1961. His death came as a complete shock to the department. (Photograph by Rollin Lane Jr.; courtesy of LFRA collection.)

Firefighters Norman Brooks and Pete Angelini are seen here manning a "big line" to control another fire at the municipal landfill on Mechanic Street in the 1960s. It was not uncommon for firefighters to spend countless hours, and in some cases days, trying to control and extinguish the fires that burned deep under ground. (Courtesy of Robert Rheault.)

Leo LeBlanc and Lorenzo "Larry" Amico find the time to smile in this 1960s photograph with the "Bread Truck" rescue in the background. In 1959, the truck was outfitted by members of the department with Scotts, axes, a cutting torch, and other tools. LeBlanc served 36 years, retiring as a lieutenant with Engine 3. Amico retired in 1985 after 31 years. (Courtesy of Robert Rheault.)

This photograph in the spring of 1968 has Alden Piper working outside the Lancaster Street fire station on engine 8, the 1933 Buffalo. He entered into the fire department in 1953 and in 1958 took over as the department's master mechanic. He was instrumental during his career in converting much of the older equipment and army surplus vehicles into brush fire trucks. (Courtesy of William Ashton.)

Lt. Arthur M. Pike Jr. retired on April 30, 1974, after more than 35 years in which he served 17 years as a lieutenant. He had joined the department as a call firefighter on February 13, 1939, and was assigned to Engine 3. Appointed a permanent firefighter on May 4, 1947, he would be promoted to the rank of lieutenant on April 9, 1957, and served as the fire prevention officer. (Courtesy of LFRA collection.)

In September 1970, firefighters began to work a 48-hour workweek using a seven-platoon rotating system. There were 73 permanent firefighters. Seen here are, from left to right, Vincent Antonucci, William Raffaele, William Penning, Deputy Chief Paul Angelini, Wayne Schofield, Robert Rheault, Deputy Chief Luigi Barassi, Marcel Remy, William Thibodeau, Bernard Jones, Gregg Hathaway, and Chief Frederick W. Johnson. (Courtesy of William Ashton.)

After serving almost six years in Vietnam with the U.S. Marines, Ronald Cormier was appointed to the department on February 26, 1974, and quickly rose through the ranks to lieutenant in 1979. On May 29, 1984, he was appointed as deputy chief with the second platoon, and he became chief of the department on May 22, 1989. He retired on May 31, 2001. (Courtesy of LFRA collection.)

On September 16, 1972, seven new firefighters were added to the permanent department, and the Leominster firefighters began working a 42-hour workweek using a four-platoon system. Assigned to each platoon were 1 deputy, 3 lieutenants, and 17 firefighters, all under the command of Chief Frederick W. Johnson. They worked two 10-hour day shifts, followed by one day off, then two 14-hour night shifts with three days off. This photograph, taken in 1976, shows the members of Group 4 in their full dress uniforms. From left to right are (first row) Thomas Jordan, Lt. Lester Cormier, Deputy Chief Luigi Barassi, Lt. Leo LeBlanc, and Lt. Charles Lowe; (second row) Roger Bigelow, Roger Caisse, Pete Angelini, John Pichette, Gerald Marino, and Larry McNeill; (third row) William Raffaelle, Ken Huckins, Ralph Wallace, Cliff Eldridge, and Roland Peloquin; (fourth row) Leo Courtemache. (Courtesy of LFRA collection.)

Alfred E. LeBlanc was appointed on June 2, 1979, and promoted to lieutenant in 1983. He was promoted to deputy chief in 1988, and was in charge of Group 2. On June 23, 2003, he took over as chief of the department. His career was shortened due to an illness, and he was forced to retire for health reasons on June 12, 2006. (Courtesy of LFRA collection.)

There are currently 80 career firefighters assigned to the Leominster Fire Department operating three engine companies, one ladder company, and a rescue company using a four-platoon system. They include a chief, master mechanic, 5 deputy chiefs, 14 lieutenants, and 59 firefighters. In 2008, the department responded to 6,913 calls. Current chief Ronald M. Pierce is a fourth-generation firefighter. (Photograph by Scott A. LaPrade.)

Firefighter Scott A. LaPrade was appointed to the department on July 25, 1989. For nearly his entire career, he has been photographing and documenting the faces and the fires of area fire departments. Much of his work can be seen on his Web site, Smoke Showing Photography. He is currently assigned to Group 4, Ladder 1.

Lt. Charles R. LeBlanc joined the department in 1973 and in 1976 joined with Deputy Chief Rosario Amico in running the EMS program within the department. His work includes documenting and coordinating a continuous EMT recertification program for the 80 members of the department. He now serves with Group 2, Engine 3. (Photograph by Michael S. LaPrade.)

Rev. Susan Suchocki Brown became the department chaplain in 1996. She is a founding member of the Massachusetts Corps of Fire Chaplains, commissioned by the fire marshal's office, and serves with the Unitarian Universalists Trauma Response Ministry. She has served at the Worcester Cold Storage fire, the site of the September 11, 2001, tragedy in New York City, and numerous other natural disaster scenes. (Photograph by Scott A. LaPrade.)

Paul F. Kennedy joined in 1965 and would be assigned to fire alarm where he became known as "Operator One" by all area departments. He was instrumental in maintaining a regional mutual aid agreement and helped to establish the 911 telephone system now in use. He kept the records for the department and has continued to do so, even after his retirement in May 2006. (Courtesy of Paul F. Kennedy.)

Firefighter Roger H. LaPointe, seen here with his father, Bernard, after a blaze in 1986, is the fourth member of his family to serve with the Leominster Fire Department. In 1986, he began his research and in 1990 authored the history of the department and was recognized as Firefighter of the Year by the Leominster Rotary. In 1992, he was given the Vincent "Chalk" Antonucci award by Local 1841. In 1996, while on a firefighters exchange program, he was recognized by the Ministry of Petrozavodsk, Russia, for heroism and bravery at a ski factory fire in Sortavala. In June 2008, he was able to reorganize and help complete the firefighters memorial honoring more than 190 firefighters and was awarded the Paul Harris Award by the Monty-Broc Rotary. Appointed on March 1, 1982, he is currently assigned as the Engine 4 driver on Group 4. (Photograph by Deborah LaPointe.)

Four

SOUND THE ALARM

This is the great fire of July 10, 1873. The fire began at about 11:30 p.m. when dense smoke and flames were discovered pouring from the rear of the Burditts Block and its basement, which was used as storage for the Arlington Piano Company. When the firemen reached the spot at Pleasant and Park Streets, the southeast end of the building was in flames and was spreading down Central Street. Five streams of water were immediately played upon the fire. (Photograph by E. G. Davis; courtesy of the Leominster Historical Society.)

The fire then spread to Pierce and Robbins stables and sheds on the west and communicated to the Hotel Block, which was soon in flames. The flames then took hold of the Arlington PianoForte Manufactory. They were unfortunate as they had a large stock of pianos on hand, nearly 200, and were only able to save 10 or 12. At several critical moments, it appeared the fire may spread across Central Street, as the Monoosnoc Hall took fire several times and all the windows in the Woods Block were broken by the intense heat. The photograph above by E. G. Davis is a view from the Woods Block building on Central Street looking toward Adams Street, with the Monoosnoc Brook to the left. The Torrent Engine Company is seen to the right of the brook, the men in action as they supply water to the firefighters of the Monoosnoc Hose Company, seen to the far right. (Courtesy of the Leominster Historical Society.)

The hotel building was a landmark, built in 1780. The fire burned on Central Street (lower part of photograph) from Pleasant and Park Streets (to the right) to a point opposite Manning Avenue. Six buildings in all were burned, destroying Monument Square all the way to Monoosnoc Brook. Two stables, the G. S. Jones Hotel Block, the Burditt Block, the Arlington Piano Block, and the Jones Block were all burned to the ground. To stop the spread of the fire, a shoe store next to the Jones Block was ordered torn down, and firefighters were able to use hooks to do this. In doing so, the fire was contained. Incredibly, no one was reported as killed or injured in the fire. The fire is believed to have started by the upsetting of a kerosene lamp and spread to hay and other combustible materials used for packing of the pianos. (Photograph by E. G. Davis; courtesy of the Leominster Historical Society.)

The Lockey building on Mechanic Street was completely destroyed in a spectacular fire on August 15, 1882. After a fire in 1861, the Lockey Piano Company next door had hose lines installed on each floor of its factory and was able to keep the fire from spreading. One firefighter was injured when he was run over by the hose carriage while responding. (Photograph by E. G. Davis; courtesy of the Leominster Historical Society.)

Rice and Holden's piano and box factory, located on Mechanic Street, was destroyed in an early-morning fire on February 12, 1894. The fire started in the two-story sawmill and quickly spread to the four-story factory building, which measured more than 100 feet in length. In less than one hour, it collapsed to the ground. (Photograph by E. G. Davis; courtesy of the Leominster Historical Society.)

The W. S. Reed Toy Company on Summer Street, makers of mechanical toys, was destroyed on February 7, 1896, in a fire attributed to electric wires. The five-story building measured 165 feet by 40 feet, and because it had been built alongside a ravine, firefighters could only fight the fire from one side. They remained on duty over 22 hours. (Photograph by E. G. Davis; courtesy of the Leominster Historical Society.)

Box 69 was sounded at 7:55 p.m. on February 10, 1898, for a fire at the corner of Merriam Avenue and Main Street in the building known as the Columbia Block. The Columbia Hotel was a popular rest stop for those traveling by train, as it faced the train depot on Summer Street. Evidence of this cellar fire can still be seen today. (Courtesy of Mildred Hirst.)

On November 14, 1898, box 69 sounded at 7:30 a.m. when a fire was discovered in a building owned by W. H. Baker and occupied by Bassett and Baker and Katherine Pigeon, known as the Water Street Bakery. When firefighters arrived, they discovered fire coming from the basement windows, and two streams of water were quickly put into use. Although the fire caused damages exceeding $1,200, it could have been much worse as the other buildings were close by. It was deemed a miracle by those there that a conflagration did not occur. The fire was deemed accidental, caused by a kettle of fat boiling over on a stove in the basement of the bakery. (Courtesy of LFRA collection.)

The Unitarian church on West Street was burned on January 12, 1903. The general-alarm fire was reported shortly after 9:00 p.m., when smoke was discovered coming from the bell deck. The steeple crashed to the ground shortly before midnight, but the Revere bell was saved and hangs today in the new church. The church had been built in 1823. (Photograph by E. G. Davis; courtesy of the Leominster Historical Society.)

The Scanlon Building at Pleasant and Park Streets received heavy damage on February 19, 1904. Box 14 was sounded at 6:25 a.m. for the Allen Block roof, and then a general alarm was sounded. Fire companies were on duty for 12 hours, but to their credit this building still stands, less the top floor. (Photograph by E. G. Davis; courtesy of the Leominster Historical Society.)

It was on February 10, 1905, that a general-alarm blaze struck the Williams and Winn Company at 85 Water Street. Box 36 was struck at 11:26 a.m. followed by 10 blows for a general alarm. It was thought that 20 people had been burned to death, but it was discovered that 17 people had been burned seriously. (Courtesy of Dorothy Shepard.)

The millroom at the Whitney Carriage plant on Water Street was destroyed on February 16, 1910. Building 1 was heavily involved in fire when firefighters arrived at box 232 at 2:55 p.m. The company was known worldwide as the maker of children's carriages, and today many are highly sought after by antiques collectors. (Courtesy of Mildred Hirst.)

One of the town's more devastating fires occurred on December 22, 1909, when the new town hall, including valuable records and papers, was destroyed. The *Leominster Enterprise* reported, "Where yesterday stood the finest town hall building in northern Worcester County today there is a mass of ruins." The alarm was received at 8:10 p.m., and a general alarm was quickly sounded. Firefighters were handicapped, as they did not have long enough ladders to get above the fire. The roof fell in at 10:00 p.m., sending a shower of sparks that for a time threatened the whole town. While some firefighters directed streams into the building, others concentrated on the Baptist church "as fire licked from time to time making the bricks so hot that the water made the building steam like a gigantic tea kettle." The building had been built in 1895. The cause of the fire was reported as being one of three causes: defective electric wires, rats and matches, or spontaneous combustion. (Photograph by Percy Johnson; courtesy of the Leominster Historical Commission.)

The first of two nearly disastrous fires at the Nickerson Block, 26–32 Main Street, occurred on April 17, 1925. At 1:40 p.m., box 14 was sounded for a fire in D. C. Nickerson's Dry Goods in the basement of the Nickerson Block. Five blows for a general alarm were sounded at 1:58 p.m. The second fire occurred on February 18, 1930, and threatened the Richardson building nearby. (Courtesy of Ronald Pierce.)

On the early morning of September 29, 1927, box 14 was called for a fire at the Music Hall Block and the Bowen and Fuller grain store, on Mechanic Street. The fire gutted the four-story brick building, which included the Hub Bowling Alley and pool and billiard hall as well as the theater. The grain store, located in the rear, was also destroyed. (Courtesy of George and Mildred Hirst.)

On Wednesday afternoon, February 16, 1938, a general-alarm fire destroyed the Central Hotel Block at Mechanic and Water Streets. Box 12 was sounded just before 1:00 p.m., and the fire, fanned by a swift wind, spread through the partitions. Firefighters donned smoke masks and went through all floors of the building to locate the fire, which seemed confined to the partitions, spreading quickly to the roof. Firefighters manned deck guns from rooftops of nearby buildings to control the fire. The block lay in the center of the city's mercantile section and was located between the Whitney Block on Mechanic Street and the Water Street garage buildings on Water Street. Its location directly opposite the Plymouth Theater building on Mechanic Street and the Moose Hall building on Water Street gave firemen considerable worry in case the blaze, which was confined and buried in smoke, should spread. (Courtesy of Russell Johnson.)

A fire on June 23, 1940, the origin of which is unknown, razed the three-story factory building formerly occupied by the Harwood Leatherboard Manufacturing Company at 279 Mill Street and owned by Fred A. Whitney. The fire was a spectacular one and attracted throngs of motorists who lined up along the dead-end streets of French Hill to see the flames shooting skyward. The structure, a wooden frame building built about 1870, had been vacant for more than 25 years, and there were no windows in it, the glass in them having been broken out. The fire, fed by the open windows, spread rapidly, and the entire structure was a tinderbox when firefighters arrived to box 48. Firefighters put their efforts into saving a home located nearby from the intense heat. Firemen reported several pigeons lost their lives in the burning building, apparently attempting to save their young. (Courtesy of Russell Johnson.)

On the afternoon of June 19, 1940, firefighters responded to this fire at 17 Lancaster Street. The fire was contained to partitions and heavily damaged the sulphur baths of John DiGrigorio and the barbershop. No one was injured. (Photograph by Felix Seliga; courtesy of LFRA collection.)

A general alarm was needed to control this fire that began on the rear porches of 155 Third Street and spread quickly to a second three-decker apartment building at 161 Third Street. The fire occurred on June 9, 1941, destroyed the Gariepy Furniture Store, and heavily damaged several others. It took firefighters nearly three hours to control the stubborn blaze, which injured three people. (Courtesy of Russell Johnson.)

Not since the great fire of 1873 had Leominster experienced a conflagration like what occurred on April 2, 1954. A raging fire of such magnitude occurred that it would forever be in the memory of those who witnessed it. An explosion blew out walls in the Castle Novelty Company on Manning Avenue at 12:15 p.m., and the fire, fanned by brisk winds, quickly spread to homes on Mount Pleasant Avenue and Wilder Avenue, destroying seven additional buildings. The blaze mushroomed, and the intense heat drove firefighters back time and again. Below, Lt. Joseph Tourigny and other firefighters work to stop the spread of the fire as it burns freely in several three-story apartment buildings on Mount Pleasant Avenue. (Above, courtesy of LFRA; below, courtesy of the Tourigny family.)

The fire was fanned by 60-mile-per-hour winds and a general alarm was sounded from box 12 at 12:20 p.m. Oil barrels containing range and fuel oil for homes in the apartment buildings were bursting and exploding, causing firefighters to seek cover. Several automobiles parked alongside the Castle Novelty building were burned as well. Every available firefighter and vehicle was on scene. For a short time, communications were knocked out, and the fire warden in the fire tower at Mount Wachusett, seven miles away, reported he could see the heavy smoke and fire. Unable to contact the dispatcher in Leominster, he contacted surrounding towns, which responded and aided local firefighters. At least 14 firefighters were injured, many escaping serious injury when the walls of the Castle Novelty collapsed. At one time, there were six dwellings afire, but quick work subdued the flames before they had gained any headway. (Courtesy of Anthony Amico.)

A grass fire on January 16, 1949, was fanned by high winds and destroyed a home at 76 Harvard Street, requiring box 41 to be sounded at 12:16 p.m. Low water pressure prevented firefighters from halting the blaze, which spread quickly when two oil barrels attached to the home exploded. The homeowners were preparing to celebrate their 25th wedding anniversary that evening. (Courtesy of Paul F. Kennedy.)

It was to become a daily routine for the firefighters of Leominster in the 1960s and 1970s to spend an entire day at the municipal dump, especially during a hot afternoon in midsummer. Over the many years that the dump had been used, various chemicals had been stored there in drums, and no one was surprised by the colors in the smoke that could be seen for miles. (Courtesy of LFRA collection.)

A grass fire spread to a home at 37 Fairmount Street on April 10, 1954. Sparks fanned by high winds apparently set fire to a wooden window frame on the third floor and quickly spread into the attic. Note the wooden ladder bending under the weight of the firefighters as they battle the fire. (Courtesy of Paul F. Kennedy.)

The 150-year-old Tuttle farmhouse on Pleasant Street was completely destroyed by fire on July 22, 1957. Firefighters were hampered in their attempts to control the fire, having to lay 3,000 feet of hose line to the nearest water supply. Lt. Donald Gillis received a back injury after the roof collapsed, yet he managed to hold the roof rafters until the men cleared the building. (Courtesy of Paul F. Kennedy.)

The DiMassa Block at 43–47 Water Street was completely destroyed in a spectacular nighttime fire on May 6, 1960. Firefighters responding to the 9:25 p.m. call found heavy fire showing from the building, threatening O'Connells Chevrolet at 23 Water Street. Firefighter Leo LeBlanc of Ladder 2 successfully drove several new automobiles from the garage's showroom. (Courtesy of Paul F. Kennedy.)

It took more than 100 firefighters to battle a three-alarm fire that took the life of a 58-year-old woman on February 22, 1961. Box 219 was sounded just after 1:00 a.m. for 32–40 Mechanic Street, followed quickly by a second and third alarm. Several people had to be rescued by firefighters over ladders. The fire caused more than $500,000 in damages. (Courtesy of LFRA collection.)

It took more than 200 firefighters from nine communities to battle a $300,000 general-alarm blaze on January 25, 1962, that destroyed the Eagles Block on Mechanic Street. Only three walls remained of the building that housed the Blue Moon Cafe and Gerry Burke's Dance Studio, as well as the Eagles Lodge and a bowling alley. The fire was believed to have started in the first-floor bowling alley and spread quickly, threatening the Goguen Block next door. Boxes 728 and 219 were struck at 11:28 p.m., a second alarm at 11:34 p.m., followed by a third alarm at 11:43 p.m. A general alarm was ordered at 11:52 p.m. (Above, courtesy of Robert Sideleau; right, courtesy of LFRA collection.)

Engine 6 appears as a silhouette as flames destroy the Rouleau barn, located at 187 Lowe Street in this May 17, 1962, photograph. The fire destroyed the barn and caused extensive damage to the home. A tractor was also destroyed. The barn was completely engulfed in flames when firefighters arrived at 4:20 a.m. (Courtesy of LFRA collection.)

A two-alarm fire at 400 Prospect Street leveled a three-story barn and caused extensive damage to a home. The fire began shortly before 4:00 p.m. on September 22, 1962, when box 142 was sounded. The fire also destroyed 30 tons of hay and killed a donkey. Two firefighters remained at the scene wetting down the rubble until 7:30 a.m. the following day. (Courtesy of Emidio Martini.)

A spectacular blaze destroyed the Spadaro barn on the afternoon of September 24, 1962. Located on the top of the hill on Union Street, it was visible for miles. In addition to the barn, 50 tons of hay was destroyed. The state fire marshal was called in to investigate the number of recent barn fires that the city was coping with. (Courtesy of LFRA collection.)

Firefighters attempt to reach the fire by ladder as it burns freely in the attic space in a three-alarm fire that gutted the interior of Alcaro's Supper House on Central Street on February 24, 1964. Firefighters battled the stubborn blaze in a temperature of 13 degrees. It took more than four hours to battle the fire, which caused more than $75,000 in damages. (Courtesy of LFRA collection.)

Two alarms were needed to control this fire at 179 Mechanic Street on November 9, 1966. The 2:27 p.m. fire began in a second-floor shed and spread upward and through the roof. Similar three-decker apartment buildings are a common sight in the city, especially in the French Hill section. Fires in this type of building are difficult to control due to their balloon construction and enclosed porches. (Courtesy of LFRA collection.)

Smoke can be seen billowing from the roof of the Fruit Growers Outlet at 738 North Main Street, during this fire that occurred on December 12, 1966. Box 515 called firefighters to the scene at 1:08 p.m. They were hampered in their attempts to locate the fire by the dense black smoke inside the building. (Courtesy of William Ashton.)

Two firefighters received minor injuries while battling a fire at V and V Plastics at 320 Central Street. The early-morning fire broke out shortly after 1:30 a.m. on November 27, 1967. The first arriving firefighters found heavy smoke pouring from all openings on their arrival. The damage was reported as being in excess of $35,000. (Courtesy of Robert Rheault.)

On January 30, 1968, while returning from another call, fire was discovered by Lt. Peter Cascio and firefighter Roger Bigelow, coming from the rear of 40 Monument Square. The multiple-alarm fire heavily damaged Montagna's Barber Shop and Maril's Shoe Repair. It was reported that 5,450 feet of hose was used in addition to 232 feet of ladders and 15 smoke masks. (Courtesy of Robert Rheault.)

The Skeeball building at Whalom Park was burned to the ground and caused serious damage to the Bowladrome on April 4, 1970. Box 6176 was sounded at 5:57 p.m., and on arrival, the entire building was a mass of flames. The building housed several game booths, including spin painting and a palm reader's booth. (Courtesy of Robert Rheault.)

A three-alarm blaze struck the Goguen Block, located at 30–42 Mechanic Street shortly after 5:00 p.m. on February 15, 1973. The fire destroyed six businesses, injured four firefighters, and caused $150,000 in damage. Smoke was pouring from the Sport Mart store when firefighters arrived. Firefighters were hampered in their attempts to attack the fire when ammunition in the sporting goods store began to explode. (Courtesy of LFRA collection.)

A five-alarm blaze ripped through the Hamilton Building of the Colonial Chateau Village Apartments at 740 Central Street on March 9, 1977. Firefighters arrived to find rolling black smoke coming from every window on the front of the 24-unit apartment building. Six firefighters were injured while battling the blaze. It had been the third fire in the complex since March 8, 1976. (Photograph by Aerographics.)

Eight people were injured, four being firefighters, as they battled a blaze at 165 Third Street on July 29, 1980. The fire started on the first floor of the four-story apartment building and spread quickly. The blaze caused more than $75,000 in damage. Firefighters were able to prevent the spread to the Inglesia Pentacostal Luiz del Mondo church located less than four feet away. (Courtesy of Paul F. Kennedy.)

A three-alarm blaze ripped through a Bay State Plastics warehouse at 40 Spruce Street early on the morning of April 24, 1981. More than $250,000 in damages was caused to the former Fuller Lumber. At one point, flames were shooting 200 feet into the air. The heat was so intense that Plexiglas windows on a building across the street melted. (Courtesy of Paul F. Kennedy.)

A fire at the former Vi's Dairy Bar, 804 North Main Street, on May 5, 1983, took the life of a Fitchburg man. Firefighters arrived to a fully involved building with flames shooting from every window as black smoke filled the early-morning sky. Firefighters discovered the body near a side door after the fire was extinguished. The $75,000 fire totally gutted the building and was ruled "suspicious." (Courtesy of LFRA collection.)

Some 11 area departments aided Leominster firefighters as they battled a five-alarm fire on February 5, 1982. The fire began in the Wiltec Company at 37 Spruce Street after a molding machine hose burst, spraying a fine mist across the first floor and igniting a molding machine. There was very little smoke showing when Chief Frederick W. Johnson arrived at 2:30 p.m., but within eight minutes, the entire building was heavily involved in fire. Firefighters, believing the fire to be contained, were checking the building for any hidden fire when suddenly fire appeared everywhere. There were 12 firefighters injured, many of them after jumping from second-floor windows when the building exploded into flames. One firefighter escaped serious injury and near death after falling into and becoming trapped in the cellar. As firefighters began to aid the injured and battle the fire, the chief happened to notice the firefighter's yellow helmet in the basement window, and he was pulled to safety. (Courtesy of Paul F. Kennedy.)

On April 26, 1986, building 5 at the former Whitney Carriage Plant, 124 Water Street, was gutted in a two-alarm fire. The first arriving firefighters under the direction of acting deputy chief Peter Cascio found heavy smoke and fire coming from every window of the four-story building upon their arrival at 2:15 p.m. The building still stands today. (Photograph by Deborah LaPointe.)

A single-engine airplane crashed landed into 17 Campbell Avenue on the night of December 26, 1986. Miraculously, no one was injured. Lt. Robert Halloran is seen here talking with the homeowner, retired deputy chief William Wheeler. In a recent five-year period, five other plane crashes took the lives of 10 people. (Photograph by Scott A. LaPrade.)

Firefighter William Bisol and Deputy Chief William "Tex" Thibodeau were two of the first firefighters to arrive at a fire that caused an estimated $50,000 in damages to a home at 209 Fifth Street. Firefighters responded at 1:10 p.m. to a call from a neighbor and on their arrival found heavy fire coming from several windows. It occurred on December 11, 1987. (Photograph by Robert Thomas.)

Four people were injured, two of them firefighters, during a two-alarm fire that heavily damaged a Prescott Street apartment house on June 18, 1989. Firefighters responded at 1:13 a.m. and found heavy fire and smoke issuing from the second floor of the three-story building. The fire caused more than $200,000 in damages. (Photograph by Scott A. LaPrade.)

The steeple of St. Cecilia's Church looms over the shoulder of firefighter Robert Sideleau II as he begins to open the roof at this fire on June 7, 1992. The fire broke out at 11:00 a.m. at 175 Mechanic Street on the third floor and spread above the ceiling and into the attic. The "all out" was ordered at 1:02 p.m. (Photograph by Scott A. LaPrade.)

Three alarms were needed to control a blaze that destroyed this building on May 5, 1994. Eight families at 66 Spruce Street lost everything in the nighttime fire that took more than three hours to bring under control. Initially one engine company had been sent to investigate an alarm, but they found heavy fire showing from all windows on the top floor shortly after their arrival. (Photograph by Richard Howard.)

The Richardson Block was struck twice by devastating fires. The first, in 1988, was a four-alarm fire that quickly spread and burned the top floor of the building. The second fire, shown in this photograph, occurred in August 1994 and went to six alarms. Lt. Robert Sideleau II of fire prevention was the first to arrive as smoke and fire billowed from the third floor. He was able to locate two residents who were unable to find their way out in the smoke. Firefighters rescued four other people after they became disorientated and lost in the heavy black smoke that quickly filled the building. The building is located directly behind the central fire station; however, crews were out answering other calls when the first call was made to the fire alarm office. It took more than 100 firefighters to battle the blaze and the heat and humidity of that August day. (Courtesy of the Fitchburg Sentinel and Enterprise.)

On May 2, 2003, a two-alarm fire destroyed a historical landmark in the city. The barn at the Sholan farm on Pleasant Street was destroyed and burned to the ground. It was more than 150 years old and was totally engulfed in flames when firefighters arrived at the scene, having been fanned by the heavy winds. (Photograph by Vincent Apollonio.)

Firefighter Gary Fournier prepares engine 8 to battle a brush fire along the railroad tracks recently. Before the housing boom of the 1980s, there were numerous areas in the city that were unreachable, and large-size brush and forest fires were common. Today's fires may not be as large as those of the past, but they are still a rite of spring. (Photograph by Scott A. LaPrade.)

Five

IT'S PART OF THE JOB

The pride of the department, the 1927 Ahrens Fox, is seen here leading the firefighters down Main Street in this late-1920s parade. It continued to run as a reserve piece until being removed from service on March 26, 1967. In November of that year, it was sold to a collector for $641. It has since been completely refurbished and can be seen at various muster events in New England. (Courtesy of LFRA collection.)

A technique of nearly all fire departments is to ladder a building as quickly as possible to ensure escape routes are available to firefighters operating inside. Today's aluminum ladders are much lighter than the wooden ladders seen in this photograph from the 1938 Hotel Block fire on Mechanic Street. (Courtesy of Kastellanos Studio.)

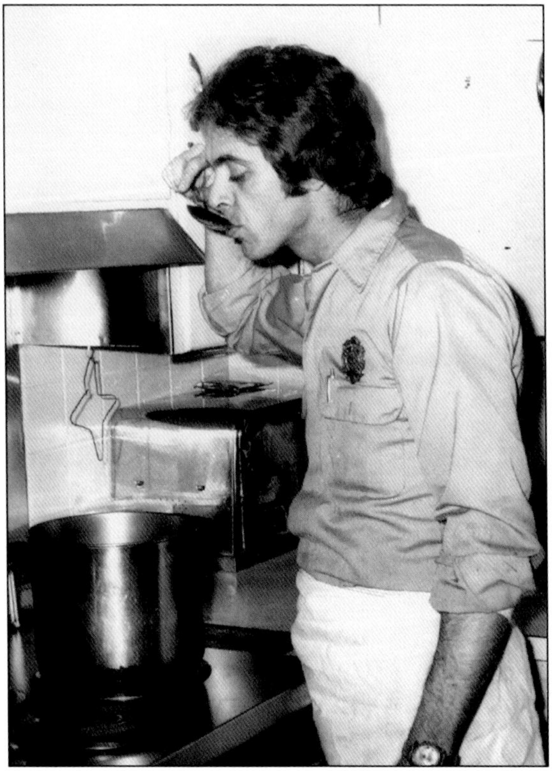

Firefighters are known to be great cooks, and the Leominster Fire Department has had more than its share, although no firehouse cookbooks have been written by this department. In this photograph from the late 1970s, Robert Thomas samples one of his specialties. In 1990, the kitchen was completely remodeled by firefighters at little expense to the city. (Courtesy of LFRA collection.)

Prior to 1931, firefighters manned the telephones in a watch booth on the stairway and alerted firefighters to calls received by telephone or public address system. On October 8, 1931, the firefighters moved the fire alarm equipment to the fireproof room at the rear of station on the first floor. On December 10, 1954, a new Gamewell fire alarm transmitter was put into service, and according to an order issued by Chief Frederick W. Johnson, "It will be the responsibility of the on duty officer to wind the transmitter, or to make certain it is wound, when coming on duty. The operator shall wind the transmitter after each box has been sounded." George Boisvert of Group 1, seen here with Chief Frederick W. Johnson, Bernard Martin of Group 2, and Leopold Thibodeau of Group 3 would be assigned as the fire alarm operators. (Author's collection.)

Returning from a brush fire on Battles Street on September 2, 1953, the 1947 Dodge forest fire truck was struck by a train and destroyed. Lt. Raymond Piper was trapped in the cab of the truck, and driver Alvin Hembrow was thrown as a result of the impact. Firefighters Vernon Miller and George Boisvert, who were both on the rear tail step, were able to jump clear. (Courtesy of LFRA collection.)

Firefighters are seen in this late-1950s photograph closing windows with brick in the rear of the fire station prior to landfill being brought in. They were filling a deep ravine to create additional parking for the growing department. Much of the upkeep and renovations at the stations are done by the firefighters. (Photograph by Rollin Lane Jr.; courtesy of William Ashton.)

An elderly man was killed in this fire at 66 Merriam Avenue on August 28, 1954. Call fire lieutenant Rollin "John" Firmin is seen here investigating the cause, which was attributed to the gentleman carrying a portable oil burner through the home when it flared up. Firefighters found the first floor of the structure fully involved on their arrival. (Courtesy of Robert Rheault.)

Carried as part of the equipment on the ladder truck since the horse-drawn days, the life net was an important tool in the event that a person had to jump to safety. In this 1960s photograph, firefighters practice using the life net in the rear of the Church Street fire station. Fortunately, there is no record of its use at a fire. (Courtesy of LFRA collection)

Lt. Peter Cascio (at left) and Lt. Walter Calamare inspect an oil burner installation as part of the Fire Prevention Bureau. The bureau also conducts inspections for smoke detectors, installs fire alarm systems, issues numerous permits, and investigates the causes of fires. (Courtesy of LFRA collection.)

Firefighter Roger Robichaud, on the left, suffered a heart attack while battling a fire at the Rockwell Woolen Mill in 1957 and was assigned to assist William Bergman, the superintendent of fire alarms, upon his return to duty. Bergman, who was also a member of the call department, was responsible for handling and maintaining the fire alarm system along with the several miles of wire that was necessary. (Courtesy of LFRA collection.)

It used to be necessary to use several electric fans to remove the smoke from a building after a fire, as seen in this photograph from the 1960s. Today's firefighters are able to use positive pressure to remove the smoke very quickly, using one fan located outside the building. By limiting the number of open windows and blowing fresh air into a building, the smoke is displaced in minutes. (Courtesy of LFRA collection.)

A tradition that most firefighters today will never get the chance to experience is "riding the back end." Nearly all trucks built since the late 1970s have enclosed cabs to protect the firefighters, but if one asked any firefighter, he would gladly take that one last ride. Seen here are, from left to right, firefighters George Boisvert, Vernon "Pete" Miller, and Rosario Amico. (Courtesy of Paul F. Kennedy.)

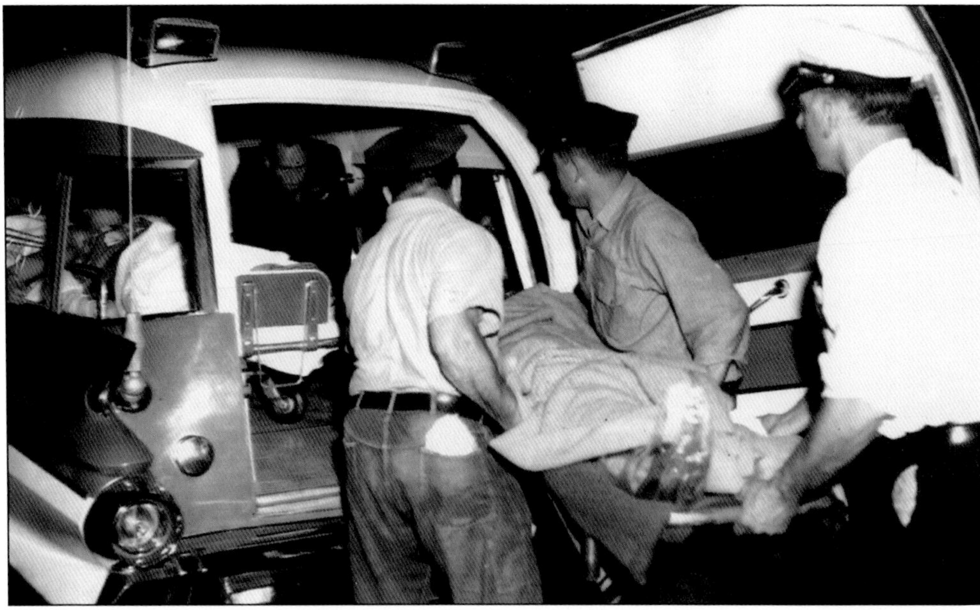

All Leominster firefighters are certified as emergency medical technicians and must maintain a rigorous training schedule. Shown here loading a stretcher into the Cadillac ambulance in this 1960s photograph are, from left to right, firefighters Norman Brooks, Larry Piermarini, and Paul Kennedy, with Lt. Felice Gabrieli. (Courtesy of Paul F. Kennedy.)

Members of the department responded to this fatal motor vehicle accident at 670 North Main Street on March 24, 1966. In the background is the bread truck, converted into a rescue truck by the members of the department in 1959. It would remain in use for nearly 20 years. (Courtesy of Roger Caisse.)

Firefighters Aime Rheault and Alden Piper and Deputy Chief James Skinner are pictured here in June 1963 on Church Street in the annual testing of fire hose. Each summer, all the department's hose is unrolled and removed from engines, curled in a loop on the apron in front of the station and tested for leaks or faulty hose, and if need be, removed from service. (Courtesy of Paul F. Kennedy.)

Firefighters turned out in the mid-1970s wearing period uniforms to draw the *Torrent* hand tub in the parade. The *Torrent* was completely refurbished by members, and at a parade in Fitchburg, they were able to spray the crowd with water. Shown are, from left to right, Archie Lefebvre, Donald Martin, Robert Cormier, Walter Calamare (with trumpet), George "Chipper" Brown, Wayne Schofield, Jimmy Smith, and Chester Pierce. (Photograph by Robert Rheault.)

Firefighter Walter Calamare, center, is seen holding a young boy who had been rescued by firefighter Gregg Hathaway, at left, after he had fallen from the bridge at the railroad crossing between Mechanic and Water Streets. Fortunately, the boy had not fallen into the Monoosnoc Brook and was uninjured after falling nearly 30 feet to a ledge. (Courtesy of LFRA collection.)

Firefighters were called to 127 Priest Street on August 5, 1964, for a reported woman in labor. Shortly after 7:00 a.m., they aided in the delivery of a six-pound, one-ounce baby girl in the kitchen of the Colcord home. Here are, from left to right, firefighters Bernie Linenkemper and John Mann, holding baby Jane, and Lt. Donald Markham. (Courtesy of Sarah Linenkemper.)

After a fire ripped through a four-story apartment house at 165 Third Street on July 29, 1980, 22 people were left homeless. Firefighter James Surovich, seen above carrying a child, and firefighter Robert Roy entered into the inferno and while searching in dense smoke heard the young girl coughing in her third-floor apartment. For his valiant effort in her rescue, firefighter Surovich was recognized by the state and the city in a ceremony attended by the young child and her mother, seen in photograph at right. The young girl, MaryLou Stoshack, was three years old at the time and now lives in Canada. She recently called on Jim, and they have since begun a renewed friendship. (Above, courtesy of the Worcester Telegram and Gazette; right, courtesy of the Surovich family.)

In January 1943, the Red Cross held a blood drive in which the men of the department participated. On the last day of the drive, the 22nd, 207 pints were collected, which was a record for the state. The week's total was 907 pints. Seen here in 1987 are, from left to right, Theresa Pixler, the director for the Red Cross, and firefighters Allan Averso and Richard Sarao. (Courtesy of LFRA collection.)

Deputy Chief Paul Angelini demonstrates the proper filling of an approved gas can in this 1960s photograph. The approved gas can must be placed on the ground before fueling, the vehicle's engine shut off, and absolutely no smoking. Today a concern for firefighters is the use of cell phones by those people fueling their automobiles. (Courtesy of LFRA collection.)

A part of the daily routine for firefighters is the inspecting and washing of the department vehicles. Seen here in the early 1980s are Lawrence "Cookie" Piermarini, Richard Sarao, and Paul Doig washing the chief's car in the rear of the station, alongside the gas pumps that have long since been removed. (Photograph by Scott A. LaPrade.)

Firefighter Robert Thomas, holding an axe, speaks to children outside the Priest Street School as firefighters Mark Matley and Jimmy Smith look on. Firefighters visit the schools as part of Fire Prevention Week in October. Stop drop and roll and calling 911 are just some of the topics discussed, but the favorite, of course, is when the children get to see the firefighters' equipment and vehicles. (Courtesy of the Worcester Telegram and Gazette.)

Firefighter Leo Enright (on ladder) is seen here with an unidentified firefighter hanging a banner for the Leominster Hospital's Building Fund Campaign in this late-1950s photograph. Today's firefighters continue to have a close working relationship with the hospital staff and assist one another with training and fund-raising. (Courtesy of LFRA collection.)

Long before the fire academy became a part of a new recruit's training, firefighters would practice their skills at the "tower" built behind engine 2's quarters on Central Street. This photograph from the 1970s shows firefighters demonstrating the use of ladders and hose lines. Since the late 1980s, newly appointed firefighters undergo a strenuous training program at the fire academy in Stow. (Photograph by Robert Rheault.)

Barbara Lancey Colburn (at left) was only four years old when her brother Raymond gave his life in the line of duty in 1924. In 2002, firefighter Kim Brown spearheaded a committee to recognize his heroic deeds by naming a street Lancey Way and erecting a granite monument to acknowledge his sacrifice. In October, in a simple service, his sacrifice was remembered, and Barbara was presented flowers by acting chief William Thibodeau. (Photograph by Paul F. Kennedy.)

Deputy Joseph Cormier sits at his desk as he enters information into the daily journal. These journals listed the firefighters on duty and all calls answered by the department for each shift. In many cases, they are the only report of an event having occurred and were the only report filed. They list the many changes in department vehicles, work done about the stations, and other little-known facts. (Courtesy of LFRA collection.)

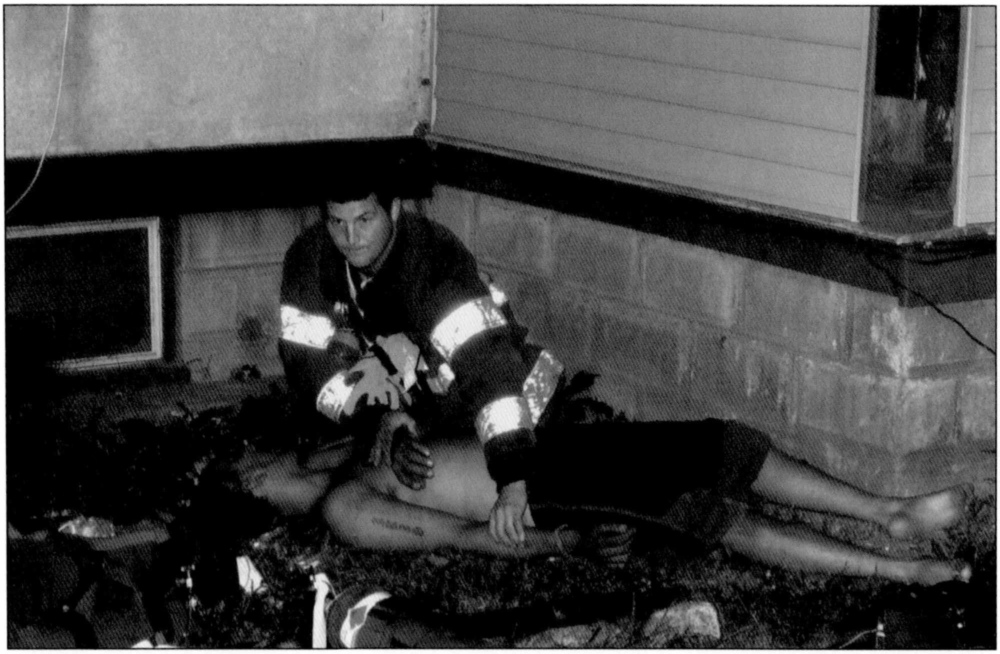

Firefighter Ryan Young of Group 4, Rescue 1, tends to a victim of a house fire on Mechanic Street. The man was asleep at the time of the fire and was found wandering outside the building on the arrival of firefighters. The victim was transported to the hospital and survived his injuries. (Photograph by Scott A. LaPrade.)

Lt. Martin Andrews and firefighter Richard Boudreau receive oxygen at a house fire on Merriam Avenue. Heat exhaustion and smoke inhalation are injuries often suffered by firefighters at a fire scene. It is also known that lung cancer and heart ailments among firefighters can be attributed to the long-term exposure to the products of combustion. (Photograph by Scott A. LaPrade.)

Much of the damage created at a fire occurs from what cannot be seen by firefighters: the fire that is hidden behind walls and ceilings that burns undetected. As seen here, the technique has remained unchanged for many years and requires the labor of firefighters using pike poles and rakes to open walls and ceilings. Today the thermal imager has become a valuable tool, as it allows firefighters to locate "hot spots," allowing firefighters to concentrate their efforts on the areas that the camera sees as excessive heat, which results in less damage. Pictured in the late-1970s photograph at right are firefighters Robert Thomas (left) and Ronald Pierce. Pictured below in 2008 are firefighter Craig Long (left) and Lt. Anthony Lefebvre. (Right, courtesy of LFRA collection; below, photograph by Scott A. LaPrade.)

On only his second day as a member of the department, rookie firefighter Robert Halloran dons scuba gear as a factory representative makes a pitch to Chief Frederick W. Johnson. Halloran joined in 1978 and went on to become a lieutenant in 1983 and deputy chief in 1987. He retired in March 2007 as the company commander of Group 4. (Courtesy of Paul F. Kennedy.)

On March 16, 2006, the firefighters assigned to Group 3 responded to a call that no one will soon forget. A 600-pound moose was struck from behind and after sliding across the hood of the automobile was found sitting in the front seat, unable to get up. Incredibly, the driver of the automobile received only minor injuries. (Photograph by Scott A. LaPrade.)

Six

TRADITIONS

In 1986, the department had in its possession one "old timer's" badge, a handful of photographs, and very few artifacts of the past. Since then, the collection has grown to include fire buckets, helmets, and nearly 1,600 photographs. Many of the artifacts now on display were given to the department by a family member in memory of a loved one. (Photograph by Roger H. LaPointe.)

Thousands of people lined the streets as part of the tercentenary parade on September 12, 1930. The event was held over a two-day period to celebrate the 300th anniversary of the founding of the Bay State Colony. Firefighters are seen here lined up on Third Street with the *Torrent* hand engine in period uniforms. (Courtesy of Mildred Hirst.)

Capt. Richard H. Cutter puts the finishing touches to a toy fire truck as a Christmas gift for a lucky child in this 1940 photograph. Today Leominster firefighters visit with those people who are confined, whether it is a young child or those young at heart, by visiting area nursing homes and the hospital and helping the U.S. Marines in their annual Toys for Tots campaign. (Courtesy of Mildred Hirst.)

Members of the department prepare for Leominster's 200th anniversary parade in 1940 with the 1848 Hunneman hand tub in this image. Seen here are, from left to right, Alvin Hembrow, Russell Johnson, James Skinner, Norman Boyden, Raymond Piper, Capt. Lawrence Paucek, and Joseph Cormier. The department is fortunate to have received two of the leather buckets seen here from Russell Johnson, son of Chief Ernest P. Johnson. (Courtesy of Russell Johnson.)

Seen here as a Boy Scout with Chief Frederick W. Johnson in 1960, Paul F. Kennedy would join the department as a call firefighter on September 26, 1965, and be made permanent in 1966. Boy and Girl Scout groups and schoolchildren are regular visitors to the firehouse to learn about the equipment and fire safety. (Courtesy of Paul F. Kennedy.)

In November 1954, firefighter Rosario Amico began a friendship with the Muscular Dystrophy Association (MDA). Working door to door, off-duty firefighters reached out to the public and collected more than $2,300. Since then, Leominster firefighters have collected well over $300,000 in their annual boot drives. (Courtesy of Rosario Amico.)

Firefighters present a check to the MDA chairwoman after their annual Labor Day boot drive in Monument Square. From left to right are the MDA chairwoman and firefighters Vincent "Chalk" Antonucci, Bernard Linenkemper, William Penning, and William Ashton. The Franklin hose reel is seen here sporting a large version of a firefighter's boot. It has become a part of every MDA event. (Courtesy of LFRA collection.)

Lester Cormier (left) and Bernie Linenkemper Jr. are seen here ringing the bell for the Salvation Army. For many years, the Salvation Army responded to fire calls to offer care to the families and coffee to the firefighters, especially on a cold winter's night. Note the air raid symbol in the upper right, a sign that reflects the period. (Courtesy of Robert Rheault.)

Smokey the Bear is well known and easily recognized as a member of the fire service. His "Only you can prevent forest fires" campaign was born in 1944. He is seen here awarding Chief Frederick W. Johnson with an award for the department's part in Fire Prevention Week. Lt. Walter Calamare of the Fire Prevention Bureau is at the far right. (Courtesy of LFRA collection.)

In the early 1950s, the Church Street fire station became a movie backdrop when members of the Leominster Cinema League produced a movie about the workings of the department. Lt. Luigi Barassi stands in front of the cameras as firefighter John Mann waits in the engine. The film was found in a box at the Leominster Historical Society and restored and is now available on CD. (Courtesy of LFRA collection.)

In 2004, Kevin "Spielberg" Morin, as he became affectionately known, spent several months with firefighters and the film *Courage Under Fire* was produced by Leominster Access Television (LATV). The film takes a look at the duties of today's firefighters and their equipment. For his part, Morin was made an honorary member of the department at the debut of the film in front of a large audience. (Courtesy of Leominster Access Television.)

In the late 1800s, each hose and ladder company had an association, which would host a concert and ball or other social gathering to raise money for their treasury. In 1893, the Hose 4 Association was formed and became the only one remaining, and they united all the companies into one. Today this organization remains in existence and hosts a dinner twice a year to reunite old and new firefighters. Seen here are those present at a meeting in 1951. From left to right are (first row) Luigi Barassi, Walter Lynch, George LaBuff, Assistant Chief Fred F. Johnson, Kenneth Swift, and Robert Farr; (second row) Albert Girardin, Elmer Wass, Capt. Richard H. Cutter, Don Gillis, John Crossett, and Ray Piper; (third row) Leo Enright, Paul Angelini, Joe Love, Felice Gabrieli, and Leopold Thibodeau. (Courtesy of LFRA collection.)

Following the sudden deaths of several members of the department during the latter part of the 1890s, the firefighters held their first memorial service on June 16, 1901. Under the direction of LFRA president Chief Charles A. Garland, the men marched through the streets and then attended services at the Methodist church. Afterward the men placed flowers at the graves of the firefighters to honor them. (Courtesy of LFRA collection.)

Chief Frederick W. Johnson leads elected officials and the members of the department down Central Street to the firefighters memorial at Lancaster and Central Streets in this 1960 photograph. The second Sunday in June is now recognized as the day when firefighters, family, and friends gather to remember the departed members of the department. (Courtesy of LFRA collection.)

Firefighter Leon Baron sits down on the tail step, exhausted and beaten, after a fire on Third Street in 1980 as his young son Lee checks on him. Lee would follow in the footsteps of his father by joining the department in 1995 and now serves as a lieutenant assigned to fire prevention. Another son, Daniel, serves with Rescue 5 in New York City. (Courtesy of Paul F. Kennedy.)

The department has had many families with several generations of firefighters and is called a brotherhood. Not since the Amico brothers in the 1960s has there been a family like the Griffins. Seen here are, from left to right, Patrick, who retired in 2007; Ronald, who is the Engine 4 driver with Group 3; and Robert, assigned to Group 4, Engine 4. (Courtesy of the Griffin family.)

After an extinguisher exploded in May 1924, killing firefighter Raymond Lancey, Fire Chief Ernest Phelps issued an order that all vehicles and equipment would be checked on a weekly basis. Since then, all department vehicles are thoroughly checked for safety and all equipment accounted for and inspected. Shown above are firefighters Raymond Melodino (left) and Norman Brooks looking over a ladder and noting the condition of the rungs and rope in a photograph from the 1960s. Below are firefighters Robert Rheault (left) and Ronald Pierce examining the tools on the heavy rescue in the mid-1970s. In addition, all ladders are tested annually by an independent agency, and a maintenance schedule of all department vehicles is kept by fire department mechanic David Comeau. (Courtesy of LFRA collection.)

During the 1950s and into the 1960s, firefighters would arrive at the firehouse in dress uniform, stand roll call, and await their assignments. Afterward they were allowed to change into their work uniforms. Pictured standing roll call in this mid-1970s photograph are, from left to right, firefighters Bernie Linenkemper, William Penning, Archie Lefebvre, Robert Rheault, Salvatore Spinelli, and Edward Comeau. (Courtesy of LFRA collection.)

The 11th Annual Concert and Ball was held at Leominster City Hall in 1961. Since the 1880s, firefighters traditionally held a concert to raise money for their treasuries to purchase much-needed uniforms and supplies. Today the LFRA uses the event to raise monies for scholarships and to aid the families of firefighters that might be in need of assistance due to illness or death. (Courtesy of Marcel Remy.)

The photograph used for the cover of this book is that of Hose Company 2 at the beginning of the 20th century. The firefighters of Group 1 in the 1970s re-creating the same photograph are, from left to right, Marcel Remy, George Boisvert, William Ashton, Deputy Chief Rosario Amico, John Picone, Jeff Olson, Lt. Roger Pierce, and William Thibodeau. On the ladder are Ronald Cormier and Gregg Hathaway (with nozzle). (Courtesy of LFRA collection.)

The firefighters of Group 3 replicated the same early-20th-century photograph in the late 1980s. Pictured in the more traditional leather helmets are, from left to right, Jeff Davis, Carl Cote, Ronald Griffin, Deputy Chief Robert Rheault, John Picone, Kevin Sideleau, Lt. Frank Masciangioli, and Tom Havey. On the ladder are Gary Fournier and Robert Cormier (with nozzle). (Courtesy of John Picone.)

On April 17, 1969, Leominster firefighters were officially chartered as Local 1841 and a member of the International Association of Fire Fighters. The above photograph is of the signing of the first agreement with the City of Leominster on May 29, 1970. Pictured are, from left to right (seated) Chief Frederick W. Johnson, Mayor Ralph Crossman, and president Norman Valois; (standing) Vincent Antonucci, Lorenzo Amico Jr., Ralph Caisse, and Francis Normandin. Below is the negotiating team with Mayor Stephen Perla (seated) signing a contract on December 12, 1989. Pictured are, from left to right, John Picone, Robert Sideleau II, Ronald Pierce, Frank Masciangioli, and Edward Byrne. (Courtesy of Local 1841.)

Local 1841 has always been active in local and state politics for the betterment of Leominster firefighters. Several of the members are seen above as the union endorses Mayor Richard Girouard in his reelection bid. From left to right are (kneeling) William Roy, Robert Sideleau, Roberto Lugo, John Picone, Kevin Sideleau, John Gendron, and Craig Long; (standing) Charles Muth, James Guilmette, Ed Byrne, Gregg Hathaway, Daniel Bouchard, Patrick Griffin, Ronald Pierce, Mayor Richard Girouard, James Surovich, Paul Doig, Mark Burnett, Ronald Cormier, and Carl Cote. In the image below, they take a moment with Congressman John Olver and Sen. John Kerry in 2008. From left to right are (kneeling) Robert DiMarzio, Carlo Altobelli, Andrew Dunner, and Deputy Chief Robert Sideleau II; (standing) Paul Doig, Congressman Olver, Senator Kerry, Travis Vallee, John Picone, and Ronald Griffin. (Courtesy of Local 1841.)

The firefighter's honor guard leads the Scots Highland Bag Pipe Band, followed closely by dignitaries and firefighters on Firefighter's Sunday in the 1990s. Firefighter William Penning, with trumpet, calls cadence as they make their way down Merriam Avenue. Members of the honor guard pictured here are, from left to right, Michael Proietti, John Gendron, Lt. Robert Thomas, Mark Burnett, and Deputy Chief Ralph Jackart. (Photograph by Scott A. LaPrade.)

For many years, even after his retirement in 1994, firefighter William Penning led the honor guard with his booming voice and cadence. In 2000, he relinquished his role and turned the trumpet over to Lt. Robert Thomas. The trumpet and duties are now in the hands of firefighter Ryan Young. (Courtesy of Robert Penning.)

Chief Frederick W. Johnson, at left, and LFRA president Alden Piper, on right, are seen here unveiling the new firefighters monument at the intersection of Lancaster and Central Streets on June 8, 1958. Prior to this time, firefighters would attend a mass and with the sounding of two blasts of the department whistles, place a wreath at each firefighter's grave. (Courtesy of LFRA collection.)

During the latter part of the 1970s, the firefighters chipped in and paid for a new firefighters monument and erected it in the square at Park and West Streets, where it is located today. Pictured are firefighters Richard Boudreau and Cliff Eldridge in 1979. Every year, on the second Sunday of June, family and friends gather to remember those firefighters who have served. (Courtesy of LFRA collection.)

After many years of planning, extensive work was done and two new monuments were added bearing the names of 192 deceased firefighters. The names engraved are those who served as permanent firefighters and retired on pension or disability, members of the call force or in the days of the volunteers with more than 15 years of service, or firefighters who died while active members. On a very hot and humid Sunday morning, June 8, 2008, Leominster firefighters led by LFRA president Robert Penning, along with more than 750 family and friends from all over the country, gathered to pay their tribute. The cost of the project was nearly $28,000 and was made possible by area businesses and donations from the families and friends of these former firefighters. (Photograph by Robert Penning.)

At the dedication of the new firefighters memorial in 2008, many members of the department took a moment to pose with 32 of the retired firefighters who were in attendance. Pictured here are, from left to right, (first row) Lt. John Gendron, Deputy Daniel Kirouac, Michael Marino, Lt. Gary Dunner, Robert Gaudet, Andrew Dunner, Seth Augat, Stephen Augat, John Picone, Anthony Amico, Jeff Nickel, Paul Doig, Shawn Phillips, Lt. Alfred Kirouac, Mark Burnett, Jeff Vaillette, Michael Voyer, John Perry, Roger Walton, Vincent Alia, Charles Muth, Brian LeBlanc, Rick Cormier, and Vincent Apollonio; (second row) Donald Preville, Deputy Robert Sideleau, Lt. Stephen Rowland, Donald Creed, Robert Penning, John Pichette, Lt. Robert

Thomas, Paul Lehoux, Raymond Cormier, Chief Ronald Pierce, Lt. Lester Cormier, Vernon Miller, Mayor Dean Mazzarella, Lt. Charles Lowe, Lt. Roger Pierce, Wayne Schofield, Jimmy Smith, Gary Frechette, Lt. Robert Miller, Lt. Leo LeBlanc, Lt. Santino Tocci, Archie LeFebvre, Jeff Gillberg, Gerald Marino, Lt. Peter Cascio, Larry Piermarini, Deputy Robert Halloran, Leon Baron, Lt. Marty Andrews, Mario Lanza, Lt. Joseph Love, Lt. Felice Gabrielli, Lt. James Surovich, Emmanuel Longo, Roland Peloquin, Deputy William Thibodeau, Kevin Sideleau, Lt. Robert Sideleau, Robert DiMarzio, Carlo Altobelli, and Lt. Lee Baron. (Photograph by Scott A. LaPrade.)

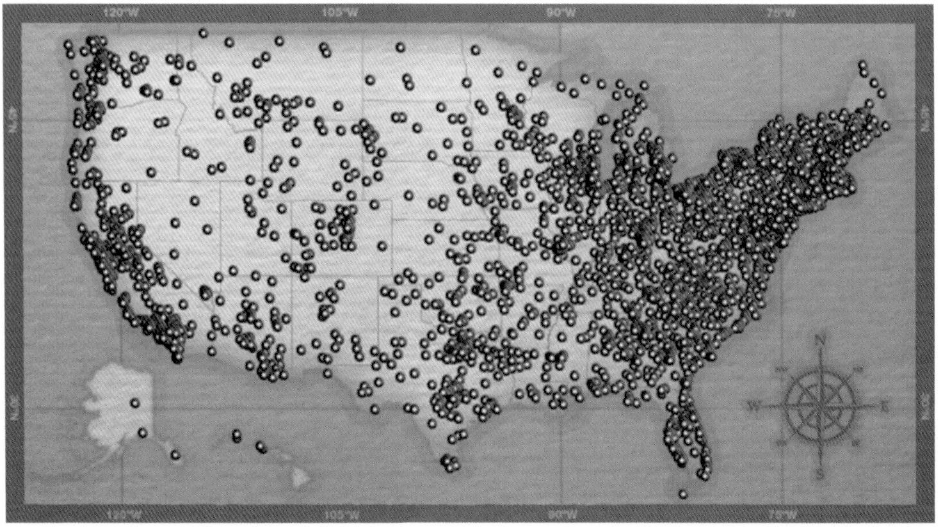